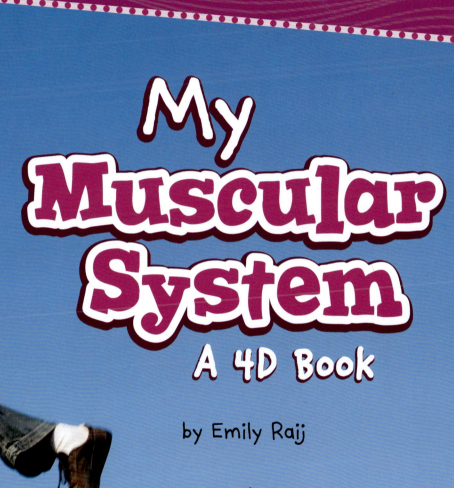

My Muscular System
A 4D Book

by Emily Raij

Consultant:
Natasha Kasbekar, M.D., Pediatrician
Kids Health Partners, LLC, Skokie, Ill.

PEBBLE
a capstone imprint

Pebble Plus is published by Pebble
1710 Roe Crest Drive, North Mankato, Minnesota 56003
www.mycapstone.com

Copyright © 2019 by Pebble, a Capstone imprint. All rights reserved. No part of this publication may be reproduced in whole or in part, stored in a retrieval system, or transmitted in any form or by any means, electronic, mechanical, photocopying, recording, or otherwise, without written permission of the publisher.

Library of Congress Cataloging-in-Publication Data
Library of Congress Cataloging-in-Publication data is available on the Library of Congress website.
ISBN 978-1-9771-0233-1 (library binding)
ISBN 978-1-9771-0535-6 (paperback)
ISBN 978-1-9771-0235-5 (eBook PDF)
Provides facts about the muscular system.

Editorial Credits
Karen Aleo and Anna Butzer, editors; Charmaine Whitman, designer; Kelly Garvin, media researcher; Katy LaVigne, production specialist

Image Credits
iStockphoto: FatCamera, 15, Milatas, 13; Shutterstock: Alila Medical Media, 7, 9, Alila_vector, 11, Anton Nalivayko, cover (inset), Fotokostic, 19, MANDY GODBEHEAR, 1, Monkey Business Images, 17, Peopleimages, 21, Rob Marmion, 5, Sebastian Kaulitzki, cover (inset), wavebreakmedia, cover
Artistic elements: Shutterstock/White Dragon

Printed and bound in China.
970

Note to Parents and Teachers

The My Body Systems set supports the national science standards related to structures and processes. This book describes and illustrates the muscular system. The images support early readers in understanding the text. The repetition of words and phrases helps early readers learn new words. This book also introduces early readers to subject-specific vocabulary words, which are defined in the Glossary section. Early readers may need assistance to read some words and to use the Table of Contents, Glossary, Read More, Internet Sites, Critical Thinking Questions, and Index sections of the book.

① Ask an adult to download the app.

② Scan any page with the star.

③ Enjoy your cool stuff!

— OR —

Use this password at capstone4D.com

muscle.02331

Table of Contents

Muscles Move 4

Voluntary and Involuntary Muscles . . . 10

Keeping Healthy 18

Glossary 22
Read More 23
Internet Sites 23
Critical Thinking Questions 24
Index 24

Muscles Move

Stretch! I touch my toes.

This gets my muscles

ready to move and work.

I use my muscles to

walk, talk, eat, and breathe!

Muscles are tissues in the body. They are made of strong muscle fibers. My muscles contract. This means the fibers tighten and get closer together.

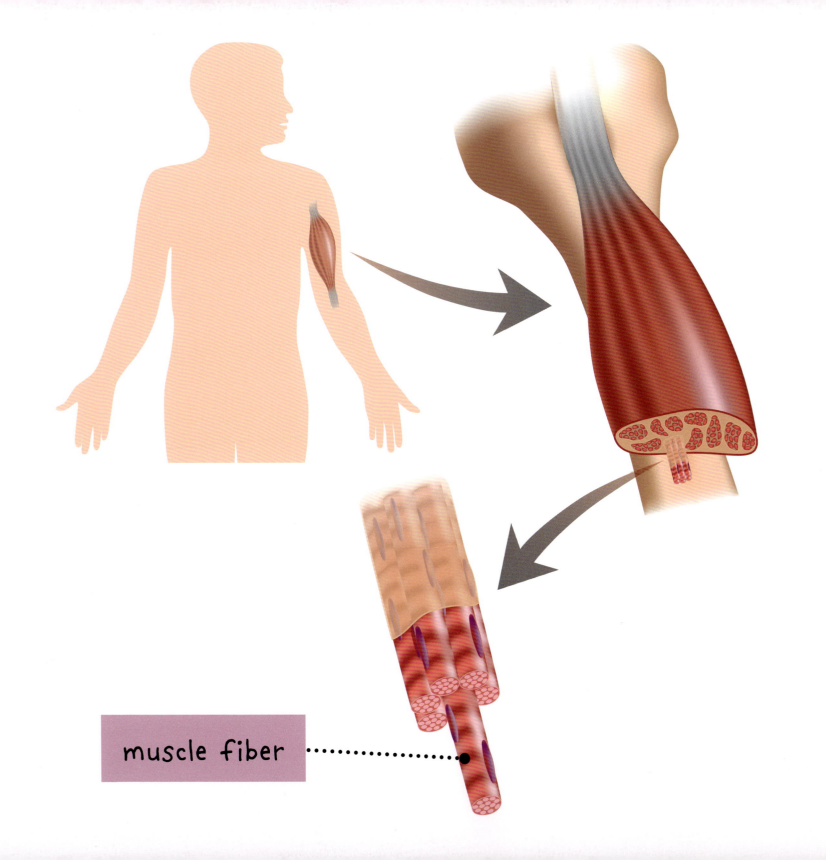

Some muscles are connected to bones. They are called skeletal muscles. These muscles move my bones. My arms and legs have skeletal muscles.

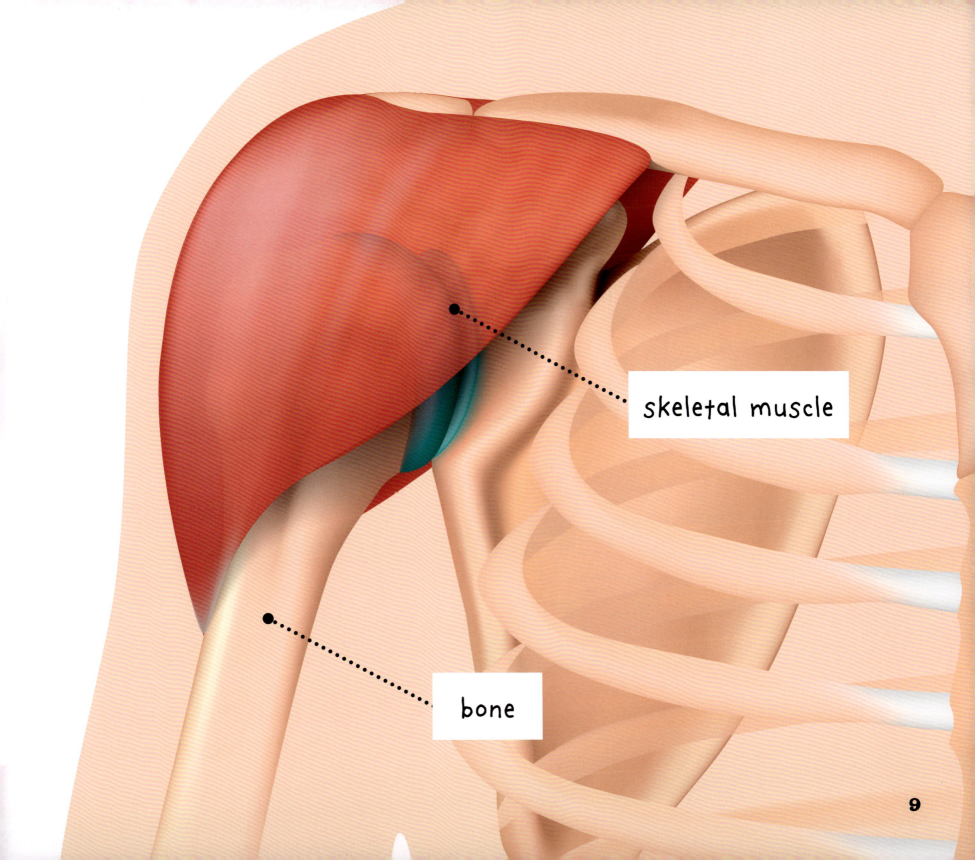

Voluntary and Involuntary Muscles

Skeletal muscles are voluntary.

I control them to move.

My heart muscle is involuntary.

It moves on its own.

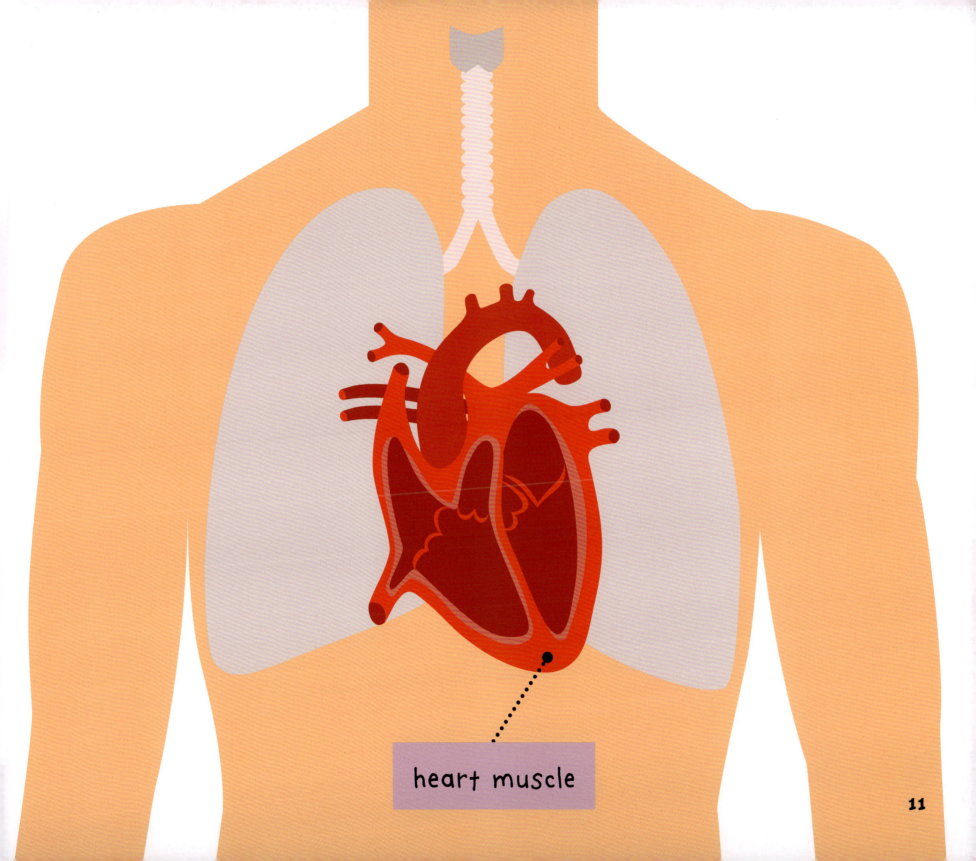

Smooth muscles are involuntary. Smooth stomach muscles help digest food. Smooth blood vessel muscles move blood in my body.

Working muscles need blood for oxygen. When I run, my heart beats faster. More blood moves around my body.

I use hand muscles to write. My brain sends a message to my nerves. Then my nerves send a message to my hand muscles to move the pencil.

Keeping Healthy

My body has more than 600 muscles, big and small. Stretching keeps my muscles flexible.

My muscles work hard. I eat healthy food to give them energy. I exercise to make them strong. I help my muscles and they help me!

Glossary

blood vessel—a narrow tube that carries blood through your body

contract—to tighten and become shorter; when a muscle contracts, it causes part of the body to move

digest—to break down food so it can be used by the body

energy—the strength to do active things without getting tired

flexible—able to bend and stretch

involuntary—done without a person's control

muscle—a tissue in the body that is made of strong fibers; muscles help the body move

muscle fiber—a long thin cell; many muscle fibers make up one muscle

nerve—a thin fiber that carries messages between the brain and other parts of the body

oxygen—a colorless gas that people and animals breathe; humans and animals need oxygen to live

skeletal—having to do with the skeleton bones

tissue—a layer or bunch of soft material that makes up body parts

voluntary—controlled and done on purpose

Read More

Brett, Flora. *Your Muscular System Works!* Your Body Systems. North Mankato, Minn.: Capstone Press, 2015.

Fittleworth, George. *Your Muscles.* Know Your Body. New York: Gareth Stevens Publishing, 2017.

Halvorson, M.D., Karin. *Inside the Muscles.* Super Simple Body. Minneapolis: ABDO Publishing, 2016.

Internet Sites

Use FactHound to find Internet sites related to this book.

Visit www.facthound.com

Just type in 9781977102331 and go.

Check out projects, games and lots more at www.capstonekids.com

Critical Thinking Questions

1. What do contracting muscles do?
2. How do involuntary muscles work?
3. How can you keep your muscles healthy?

Index

blood, 12, 14
bones, 8
exercise, 20
fibers, 6
involuntary, 10, 12
nerves, 16

oxygen, 14
skeletal muscles, 8, 10
smooth muscles, 12
stretching, 4, 18
tissues, 6
voluntary, 10